Time Sensitive

By

Julie Bolt

for my parents

Author's Note

The majority of these poems were written between 2021 and 2023. During that time, several were first published or accepted in journals and print anthologies. I'd like to acknowledge them here:

Beat Style Love Poems: A National Beat Poetry Foundation Anthology, "Homeland Security"; *Brownstone Poets Anthology 2023*, "Manahatta"; *The Celestial Review: Cycle 6*, "Dispersion"; *Club Plum*, "Time Sensitive"; *Home Planet News*, "Breathe Louder into Silence" and "Reckonings"; *Mutha Magazine*, "When I Met Him"; *Natural Worlds: A National Beat Poetry Foundation Anthology*, "Make Me a Tree"; *New Generation Beats Anthology*, "Why We Dare"; *New Verse News*, "The Day the Bombing Began"; *Open Sky Poetry Anthology*, vol. 1, "Rubrics"; *Our Changing Earth*, "The Desert Holds Me (reprint); *Shot Glass Journal*, "Remember" and "The Riverbed"; *The Raven's Perch*, "The Faithful, 1986" and "Echo Box"; *Red River Review*, "Appetite of a Dead Connoisseur"; *When Women Speak, vol. 1*, "The Desert Holds Me" and "Writing Beyond" (reprint); *Scissors and Spackle*, "The Beaded Women"; *Writing in a Women's Voice*, "Writing Beyond"; *ZOOAnthology*, "Leilani."

Table of Contents

ONE

Time Sensitive

This poem is tipping at the tipping point

Written in the era of magical thinking

 After insurrection and indictment but before conviction

Written in the age of mask wearing and mask shunning

This poem doesn't know if Amurika is liberating or going
full cheese MAGA

This poem was shot through a Texas gun and the poem
destroys guns

Written in the age of choosing our pronouns and of
Atwood's prophecy

After our first Black president but before our first woman
or queer president

This poem knows that this is how fear and change are
made

Written in children's afterbirth and in between gaps of
justice

After #BlackLiveMatter but before reparations

This poem is in on Turtle Island, demands land tax to the
Tribes or has a one-way ticket

This poem collects questions, rage, and incomplete answers, seeking recipes from scrolls

Written in starlight but soaked with blood, no more blood

After the solutions have been cataloged but before we rose and rose like we never rose

This poem will soon be dated and hopes to fade in flickers and the specs of springtide

This poem wants to scream in uproar and die amongst the warriors for utopian gleams

The best things in life are free

Except health care, land and airspace

The moon, however, belongs to everyone

but mostly the Americans, Chinese, and Russians

The stars? They belong to everyone

who uses the International Registry

because the flowers in spring, the robins that sing

the sunbeams that shine, they're yours, and they're mine

some of the time

the best things in life are free

Why We Dare

(To all youth climate activists everywhere.
Inspired by Greta Thunberg's speech at 2019's Global
Climate Summit)

Our histories are written in the dirt

The Earth remembers, while burning warning, bleeding dry

The black snake is engorged

The complicit make backroom deals, flash the hollow smile

Distract us with deep fried shit and curly fry lies

The Earth shirks and demands

"Who loves capitalism more than me?

Who loves fascism more than me?

Who loves empire, militarism, xenophobia, transphobia,

factory farms, rote miseducation, deforestation more than me?"

Aloha Honolulu, while Mauna Kea's children still hear coqui and ancestors' ghosts

Arrivederci, Grand Canal, medieval city of splendor, commerce, and song

Au revoir, Preservation Hall, Bacchus, Orpheus and Endymion, resurrected from the deep

Bangkok is sinking, Kolkata is sinking, Miami is sinking, Savannah and Ho Chi Minh are sinking

How dare you! *Fiji and Nauru,*
How dare us! *Solomon and Vanuatu*
How dare I! *Maldives and Tuvalu*

This is all wrong, so we dare what the Earth demands of us

To use our poems, science, anger, inspiration, workers, warriors and healers

Twenty-six years' time in devotion to dirt, water

For it is the absolute birthright of each generation

to name the birds, see the stars, walk barefoot and drink in rivers

Sod

Fresh Earth, pulling flesh
Plucking birds, the cleave
Pots simmering the truffles
The wheat, the potato, the leek

We are your echoes
Your heartbeats
Your dry, desolate planes
Driven by thirst and by hunger

The thought that hardens
The hand that sculpts
The neck that bends to be stroked
The eyes that close for redemption

In free expression
Fulfilling your passions
We are mayhem and madness
We are your mountains of moaning

We are made of your sacrifice, devotion and tending

We are made of your cheating, killing and lying

All passions, all intelligence, all ignorance

From that, from sod, we are made

Each generation half-blind

Pulling and pushing

Each will choose whether to survive

To give enough care and attention

With enough stubborn love, enough radical love

With enough sankalpa breaths

As atoms travel and fuse into the sod

For an unforeseen future and the impossible void

Uprise

Everyday

  resistance

    of the mind

      s t r e t c h i ng

Everyday

    resistance

      of the body

        holding space

Words that grow

      gardens

   inside souls

Revolutions that grow

       rivers

   inside minds

Feeling the fissures of new

     movements

Real shifts,

        imperfect and

                messy

Yet ignited,

      tragically,

            horrifically

      Yet ignited,

              finally

Mitigating

      language

         and space

Realigning truth

      with remembrance

In the midst of curdling

      hate groups

         police lethal terror

      encroaching

           fascism

      an actual insurrection

In the midst of the wildering

      hunger for "end days"

Orwellian curfew

   lockdown

     loneliness

   and loss

In the midst of manufacturing

  flagrant hypocrisy

    and laden lies

  Despite

    the deadly

  virus

    of the body

  In spite of the

     s e r p e n t i n e

    virus of

    the mind

  It was

    overtime

    It's been overtime

It was time

  It will be time

   For uprise

How Things Should Have Been

A young woman spends days saving lives as an EMT, ERT and a Practicing Registered Nurse. One day she may have her own practice. Meanwhile, she tends to wounds and saves lives. She is also a daughter, big sister, godmother, friend, and girlfriend. Because of her work, she sleeps at 8pm. She wakes up to work for the people's health at sunrise.

A dad, mechanic and former city-employed horticulturist struggles with asthma. He provides for his family of eight. Mornings are busy. Routines. Mouths to feed. Hugs. He takes jobs that let him breathe, is friendly with neighbors, sharing stories, selling loose cigarettes. In time, it is sunset. Time for dinner with family, including his beautiful namesake.

Her new job is a dream come true. She has been hired as a community outreach coordinator at her alma mater. She had a scholarship for the marching band. Now she will give back, mentor, and build. She already fights for the youth and against brutality using social media. Today the sun shines on her and all her good works for the future, with platforms to fulfill them for decades.

His backpack is empty when he starts classes at Bronx Community College. But the semester proceeds. He accumulates books for different subjects. Notebooks, pens, packs lunch. He works for the campus's "Future Now" program. The semesters roll by until he wears his green and black robes. He turns his tassel and goes off to meet his dreams.

Children. Children linger in grandmothers' gardens, have parties, and play with toys in the streets. In the sunshine. That's community.

After sunrise, young men and middle-aged men go to convenience stores for supplies or snacks. They leave. The day proceeds to unfold with human connections, work and leisure and passion. A young man plays the violin, even at animal shelters, for the lonely and innocent. Another performs spectacular superhuman feats on his skateboard. Young men flying! Creating art! Crystalizing life's forever moments in photos. Oh, to live, to strive and feel a calling in the chest!

A teenager strolls to his father's house. A gated community. He chats with his girlfriend on his phone. Carefree, he pops Skittles in his mouth. Sips cool ice tea. He turns his key. Then throws out the empty bag of Skittles. He places the bottle on the counter. Whispers "good night" to his girlfriend. Crawls between cool sheets.

He wakes up to blue skies. Sunrise.

The Mud Season

We stopped listening to trees

Pass the Nemifoff Vodka

We are scared, overworked, and sinking

There are bombs again, there is ash again,

Too much blood again

Young soldiers face the mud season

Slogging through Donbas

forced to commit atrocities

Wreckage, ash, fumes

Fire, clay

I will find clay, spread it thick

on my body. Roll in it

We are all clay, ideas from Earth

confused and unformed until we learn the shapes

of sovereignty, the textures of peace

In Praise of Deoxyribonucleic Acid

Dear fellow organisms,

I write today to praise thee, to praise us
To give homage to deoxyribonucleic acid

Praise to the slug, tentacles towards light and smell,
laying eggs in loam and clay

Praise to the fierce mother cow, curious,
bounding with joy, then oppressed by machinery

Praise to the cat, whisker detectors, pricked ears,
swish of the tail, the curved and pointed claw

Praise to the tree, sturdy, branches reaching,
leaves of poems, the knowledge of roots

Praise to our deoxyribonucleic acids
Parallel and unparalleled strands

spiraling into the Gaudiesque

double helices. The shapes

of biology, of physics and art

I praise us all!

Endless animation, variation, imagination

An ongoing sequence of intelligent creation

Organisms -- each intricate evolution

Connected and resonant, molecular revolution

The Day the Bombing Began

It was an East Village debacle:

Veselka, Kiev, or Ukrainian National Home

Veselka was busy and bright

Kiev was for neighborhood regulars, early or late night

UNH was to time travel into a Ukrainian private club from

another age

I loved them all, but especially Kiev

For the best comfort food in Greenwich Village

And largest portions and lowest prices

And latest hours, the most tolerant waiters

However, it was hard to decide whether to order:

a combo blintz and pierogi

or assorted pierogi platter

or savory potato pancakes

Ideally, friends would share kasha bow tie pasta,

And then there was the challah bread of clouds

with squares of bright yellow butter,

And oh the boys had crushes on the Ukrainian waitresses

And the head waiter flirted with my mom

Her cheeks flushed like borscht,

And I went so often the owner sometimes gave me a free cherry blintz!

I don't remember if I thought about when

the Greenwich Village Ukrainians

escaping Soviet oppression

But I do remember that December 26, 1991

was a joyous day. People became free, and Empire fell

I had just moved to Philadelphia

So I could not celebrate in Kiev and had to settle

for a vegetarian hoagie heavy on fried onions

Gorbachev had the map of peace on his forehead,

unlike Putin's face of war

After Philly, I moved to perfumed deserts and craggy rocks by oceans

In 2005, I returned to NYC, ready to feast on Kiev's sauerkraut pierogies

slathered in the greasy onions, applesauce and sour cream

But new ownership had resulted in Ukrainian-Asian fusion,

Small portions, aspiring to expensive tastes

And Veselka acquired long NYU lines

So I decamped to The Ukrainian National Home

It wasn't long before Kiev shut its doors forever

I will always mourn the closing of Kiev

I hope the original owners did not miss,

the entire brief window of Ukraine's democracy

Where are they now?

What are they thinking?

Putin professes the dissolution of the Soviet Union

was a myth, although those of us who were alive

experienced it, documented it, celebrated it

Now our friends are dying in the crossfires of lies

The blue sky grows dark, but the sunflowers grow

How to Make a Better World (with Standpoint Theory)

We have to decide whether we want

to just get it together

Or not

Aware of our limited standpoint perspectives

most of us can grow ourselves and water others

Our experiences learned in community and solidarity

In hunger, injustice, resilience

All these are powerful paths

Bravely generous to oneself and others

Each of us a world of unknown, unspoken mysteries

A stuck world, a liberated world

Whole galaxies out there

and in here, hidden

tentatively waiting to produce magical matter

Time for Reparations!

Pay land tax to indigenous peoples!

Consume less! Worship water!

Let truth be in the open air

Ask for preferred pronouns

Assume less. Read whole books

We are all sovereign beings of many cultures

Within and beyond time and all distant relations

Support young leaders of integrity

who represent the under-represented

Fight for rank-choice voting!

The gift of voting your beliefs

Without being rendered a thief

Stand with the suffering

Hear the accused

Watch out for misinformation and misdirection

Who owns a given media? What else do they own?

Synthesis from many sources and experiences to discern

Apply our best green practices

Enjoy a sunny day and clean a beach

Raise the roof for rooftop gardens

on horizontal buildings

Local, affordable, fresh, organic

Free rent or tax breaks for tenders

Honor all planters, pickers, the transporters

Have *si se puede* for dessert

Dance it off under the starlight

All dancers, styles, expression

Sing with all who want to sing

We all have music in our chests waiting

to bloom succulents, berries and the funkiest flowers

Represent and teach banned books!

Upgrade the youth, flip the class

Problem-pose, laugh together, co-create

Ask why we ever, ever created guns,

bombs or nukes

The answers will be forthcoming!

But will they ever be sufficient?

Child, parent, elder, limb, ash,

history's deep furnace

Dream the Possible Dream!

Turn in the guns!

Melt guns into sculptures

of humans' casting off domination,

lifting each other upward, foreheads touching, eyes

meeting

Restorative justice, distributive justice

And sometimes, retributive justice

See the horizons, the short path, the long road

Astral projection, the difficult questions

Stroke the dog or cat who needs you,

Protect the sheep, cow, pig, the aching ox

Explore the ecological necessity

of Earth's other species

Watch them see us, fellow travelers all

Forgive? Yes, it is the hardest

Forgive for one's own peace

Harder and braver, make real amends

Even if rejected

these are seeds of healing,

stepping in the grace of surrender

Start anyplace you see no stars

Start any place there is ecological decline

or human grief

Start anywhere that makes sense for you
And for all that you do, have done:
Thank you

We know so many of the answers
Yet the Earth bleeds oil for robber barons
Money isn't real
It is an idea with consequences
It is not of the Earth or for the Earth

Find wisdom in old songs and new questions
The fluid, non-binary, neurodivergent
The ten dimensions of superstring theory
Knowledge and language from other cultures
The Four Directions, The Four Agreements

We know the science of sustainability
Yet hold out hope for a miracle
Yet no passing everyday-day
No daydreams, no avoidance
No Half-Time, Minecraft, Fat burger
will eradicate what we decimate

We have to decide

We have to decide

To listen, to learn, to cooperate

To lead with love for the future

Otherwise, there is only hopelessness,

sorrow, hate and indifference.

Sacred beings, we have to decide

in vast numbers, with multitudes

of voices and spaces

consider new ideas and those

already sidelined for profit

We have to decide:

Whether we want

Whether we want

Whether we want

to get it together

to just get it together

to get it together

Or not

Echo Box

Locked down, bogged down, knocked down
Invasive thoughts on speed dial
Scrolled my timeline, switched to the hotline

Breath: breathe
Sleep: come deep
Shun shock, take stock
Hold firm on this swerving earth rock

Okay, maybe not today
Tomorrow, await
These cells will regenerate:

To feel the world and understand the stages
To teach and learn in my magic classes
To embrace and own my choices
To put gnarly ghosts down with a merciful sword
To revel in raw human company and nature
To stop apologizing
To hug my son and show him how we survive
That we get up
Just that
That we love ourselves
We choose

The Desert Holds Me

The desert moon is full and bright. The ancient properties are louder than the loudest cities. I love to wander and roll in its pink perfume, dusted by the sands of Earth's ancient peoples, of pagans past and present. The desert moon pours its light on all its life. Lush succulents hide water sources. The scampering lizards, the big-eared hare. The mourning doves sing, and desert owls emerge curiously from their holes. At night, coyotes roam and commune with haunting tones. When my mouth dries, there is the meandering Rio Grande, beckoning with seasonal flowers.

Life announces itself in the barest places. The smells of marigolds and sage rise into the air. Yellow, orange and reds stubbornly flourish. The wind whispers, and a new universe beckons. A howling as night-life awakes. The desert surrounds me and holds me. All else is small. The desert surrounds me. Pull down the clouds. The desert holds me. Pull down the rain. Rain to soothe the thirst of rabbits. Rain serenades the mountains. Pull down the clouds for Ceremony.

Comrade, two-spirit, woman, man, child, let's roll down the dunes. Become one with mud in rain, sand's perfume. Give ourselves over to everything before us. Join together with these specks of eternal time and flashes yet to come. Yes, I abandon the clock. I step into this calling. If you join me, we can face the cold nights, withstand the floods, and surrender ourselves to an unpeaceable world. I draw you towards me: towards my breast, towards forever, towards greater-than-love, towards yes, towards lark and wren, towards cactus flowers. The desert holds me. I hold you. Friend, lover, mate, sand, moonlight, winds, sky of stars, yes.

TWO

The Faithful: NYC, 1986

Fifteen, and the skinhead near Union Square baptizes me
He spits cheap wine on my face, hair, eyelashes
Soggy and foul, I become
a disciple of defiance, sorrow, blight

Daedalus journeys from Palladium to Bard
wearing AIDs
He offers me a yellow rose
I refuse then meet his ghost

Veteran Mike, homeless, burns a fatty
on the steps
of St. Mark's Church
his rambling riffs scorch the New York sky
with Saigon blood

The mohawked barmaid at Danceteria falls
Into the elevator shaft, she falls to her death
wailing all the way down:
"Degenerate the faithful with that crazy Casbah sound..."

Homeland Security

I took off my bra and waved it

lasso style around my head

My husband laughed and said,

"You're in the wrong business

You should a been a show-girl!"

Which is funny because I come from show people

and I am tone deaf with two left feet

But that doesn't stop me from doing

my hip hop hippy spin-me-right-round-baby

dance every chance I get

My husband was a downtown DJ and a dancing legend

in times of the roped off clubs, the decadence aughts

One night a bouncer friend snuck him

Into the Michael Todd Room at the Palladium

for Prince's Purple Rain Party after-party

and Apollonia approached him, and they danced

He gyrated up, and down, and did the splits

Prince did not appreciate this whole situation

And my schoolmate, now husband

was escorted out of the Michael Todd room

But all was good, all was great
because that night his mother hadn't given him money
to see the Purple Rain concert at Madison Square Garden!
Yet he despondently rode the subway with
us concert goers, staring into space
All I can say is that it was sad
So, we were all impressed
with how he turned that night around!
But that is not the point of this poem
After my husband delighted in my lasso bra dance

I leapt on the bed to squeeze and tickle him
I notice his "Original Homeland Security" t-shirt
The one with Geronimo and other Apaches
I hadn't seen this shirt in a while
So, I squealed, "OG Homeland Security!"
With his eye mask now on and almost asleep,
he chuckles and peaks through his shades,
because he thinks I said, "Old Man Security"

Yeah, Gen X is getting up there
True, we don't all hear as well as we used to

We can't all just bust out the splits

But we are still good or bad dancers, actors, comics

Sexy and gorgeous in our hard-won imperfections

Secure in our borders of us, regaling in laughter

For our favorite audience of one

Marigolds

My parents breathed theater like fire
Supernovas departing their hometowns
Blooming gold for Broadway brilliance
Characters resurrected from others' imagination

Oh, those halcyon days
Of flared pants and parties
The breezy nights of chain smoking
My asthma flaring

Debates among hungry thespians
and future producers
Straddling our brown butterfly chairs
Big ideas, big words, raucous gestures

The curtain: me backstage, restless
A beleaguered stagehand fretting
My toddler's mind absorbing
The river of words and worlds

The character, the line, the scene

Seed thoughts traveling the speed of light

I learned actors are bigger than life

Theater is the only life

Matinee brings Godot and evenings

bring Gamma Rays

Estragon says, "I'm like that.

Either I forget right away

or I never forget."

Tillie: "This part of me was formed from a tongue of fire
that screamed through the heavens until there was our
sun."

"... Atom," she said

"What a beautiful word."

Breathe Louder into Silence

She insisted on living alone
unable to breathe without labor
attached to oxygen and feeding tubes
unable to walk without trembling
coughing the thick mucus in her hardened
lungs that turned against her
twice: first her lungs, then the donor's lungs
and, gasping for air, she insisted on living alone
after drunken revelries, after work, despite
the orders of doctors and common sense
as a stagehand or playing with a band

Singing, croaking, shouting, enraged
with lungs that belonged to a quiet woman,
who was patient, loved chocolate, and now
my friend cursed a little less, licked chocolate,
but couldn't chew, there was no appetite
only startling emaciation of the cheeks, legs, and arms.
And she insisted on living alone
despite her parents' pleas for hospice

offers their own sterile care

and, yes, she was lonely; she said so

I traveled for a final visit

We watched *The Matrix, Rushmore, Behind the Music,*

pontificating about alternate realities, childhood dreams

and the virtues of Henry Rollins

She cursed cheerfully, coughing her subterranean

cough – and I flew back to LA, the final goodbye

except for a belabored phone call

when she told me the miracle

Her greatest love returned

That breakup was ugly, fueling her stubborn rage to live

The woman had left her for a simple man,

leaving her with foreign lungs, half-written songs

false breath -- and she insisted on living alone

until the lover returned with knit sweaters, tears, caresses

of mourning and elation, kisses of absolution and

of what could have been, and she heaved, asphyxiated

gasping in those last caresses, yielding in her own bed

her lover's arms, no more gasping

Appetite of a Dead Connoisseur

Memory:

When I was nine, I rang Seymour Britchky's

downstairs apartment asking for

an egg. He retorted:

"Egg? Me?

Food critic for The New York Times?"

and turned brusquely, slamming the door

I stood there stunned for minutes

Fact:

My husband is frustrated

by my ongoing predilection for ordering

and eating out, much like Seymour Britchky;

I never have an egg

Fact:

Seymour once wrote,

"Sardi's most famous dish

Is its cannelloni,

Cat food wrapped in noodle

And welded to the steel ashtray

In which it was reheated under

Its glutinous pink sauce

Memory:

When I sold Girl Scout Cookies,

Seymour purchased six boxes of thin mints

Plus fourteen peanut butter patties

I met my Girl Scout goals

Reflection:

Beard and bowtie,

Belly bordering on the rotund

But only bordering, since Seymour

walked, walked everywhere, swiftly

Memory:

Seymour sneered at my friends

hanging on our Greenwich Village stoop

With tallboys, hidden joints, and bad posture

He seethed to my mother, "They are thugs"

Embarrassed, she tried to shoo them away

Did they not know we were hungry and hopeful?

Fact:

1) In New York Seymour was known for:

a) Literary flourish and acerbic wit

b) Pissing off chefs

c) Really, really pissing off chefs

2) In June 2004, Seymour died of pancreatic cancer at age 73

3) Despite his constant presence on paper, in the city streets,

and his name clearly placed in our building directory,

City Hall has no record of any persons in New York by the name

of Seymour Britchky

Reflections:

I'm back to my vacant childhood home

after a decade of desert, ocean, mountain, sky

Back to the simmering souring city I love

I expected to see Seymour weaving through streets

Sneering and smiling, greeting, rebuking

Because he is this building, this block

All the contradictions of this place

Memory:

Seymour beamed each time

He passed our dog, Skippy

On those rare days, he greeted us:

"Flight of angels!"

Defense:

Seymour's dead, but oh

We are both hungry, greedy, hungry

For brioche, thin mints, provocations, trout almondine

Angels in the form of smiling dogs

Hungry for roast squab and squabbling,

Greedy for the name in print

Even when it's a pseudonym, and upon death

There's no proof of existence, only footprints

From Mojave to Café Loup on West 13th

Where I just passed, and Seymour Britchky,

Or whatever his name was, often drank alone

Summer Heart

(For Jamie, daughter of the Pied Piper of the Summer of
Love)

We leap over volcanoes,

enact novels, create characters

for our intricate games

We read and guess numbers and colors from each other's

minds

Your stories are four-dimensional

Your green eyes cast poems

Your laughter fills the room, street, meadow

Neither knows if we will be here too long

So, we run, run through seasons

as characters. We kiss, touch

You smell of your middle name, Heather:

spring dew, musky, alive

You sleep in a bed of musical notes,

the literal daughter of Woodstock

with the imagination to spin words

into worlds into galaxies

You miss your mother

Are you with your mother?

Are you riding in the Californian moonlight,

dashing to the stables?

Will you ride horses to the stream?

Swim naked, splashing each other

Gliding phosphorescent

under lily pads until the dawn?

You are sixteen

I step into a body outside of time

We twirl and swirl until we collapse, entangled

joined by lost companions in their radiant youth

There will be guitars by the olive trees

There will be mirrors

Let's wear purple lipstick

With glitter for sure

When I Met Him

Tuesday. The social work arrives at Los Angles Park. He scrambles out of the back seat and laughs excitedly. He inspects the bag with the stuffed elephant, Spider-Man ball and Tonka truck. His eyes turn to the grassy park, and he wants to run. We follow. Catch me. Gales of laughter. So little. Strong. Catch me. Over the rubber hills. So fast. Catch me. Gales of laughter. Up and down the slide. Catch me. Climbs the jungle gym. Caught him. Screeching laughter. The laughter morphs into tears. Walk back to the social worker: the stuffed elephant, Spider-Man ball and Tonka truck. Soft truck sounds. Tears and soft laughter. Departs with the social worker and toys.

Thursday. A knock at the door. The social worker and my new son. Observant, vigilant, delayed in speech, almost four. All his belongings in two bags. We are not the first or second home. Somber and proud. He marches in. Squinted eyes inspect pictures on the walls. The furniture. Goodbye to the social worker. Scrunches face. Cries. Let's play chase. Run. Catch me. Gales of laughter.

The Riverbed

Our car broke down
in the riverbed of the Mojave Desert
and our cell phones didn't work
and nobody was around

for miles, miles miles

I wished I was alone, lost
in the desert so I could perform
my imagined ceremonies for eternity
Hearing coyotes, seeing the stars

We sought shelter under the car
After hours, the "America First" tow truck
arrived as we frantically ripped off
our "No Blood for Oil" bumper sticker

We drank the last sips of water
I inhaled, relieved that my family

Would not die in such a tragic
and thirsty way

As we are towed, I felt yearning, guilt
for I knew that this was one missed
destiny and all else would be
smaller than imagined

Guard the Story

Love isn't dancing through moonlit lush gardens

But climbs up steep craggy mountains

A fabric of memories textured

A long look into a vibrating tunnel,

squinting late in the night

If there are decades of Love,

there are years of solace, often years of pain

But Love forgives and grows

It won't remain the same

Walking the outskirts of Love is a path

with peonies that burst

Swimming in its water is a sea of delight,

a respite –

but beware, the undertow is always there

When suffering comes,

Love pulls into the reaches

When Love's body hurts,

Love is weighed down by overload

Stay afloat!

Or don't...

Maybe you will sink with Love,

or sink without

Sometimes life comes roaring to shatter Love

And Time is something Love will hungrily take

And sometimes "love" is fake

But after stitching, cleansing and respite

Love may once more extend a hand

And together you will swim backstrokes

with Love in clear waters

To other worlds

in the company of Love – and *as* Love

Defying palettes in the neon colors of the deep

Of all longitudes and latitudes

Let Love itself bear witness to the story

Guard the story

Make Love an epic story,

a tender story

a story that enfolds

into the larger world

with private creases

tucked within the story

Accept compliments with humor

and reject judgment of Love's grace

Love is no one's possession

But its own teethed and silk-bound beast

Felt on the skin, in the muscles, deep in the bones

Many of the lucky dance with themselves

in their own singular and beautiful ways

Smiling near your twirling laughing shadows

Through Love's gift

of unpromised days

A Cat Moves On

She stands over his body

Smells his fur, nose, mews gutturally

Her body is warm, his is cold

She is asking something

The dog is not coming back

Now she assumes his jobs

Waits for us at the bathroom door

Greets us on arrival

Claims my husband's lap

Sleeps in stillness, not like death

Ears flick, long tail curled around her

She is deep in animal dreams

Far from the small human world

The dog is not coming back

The Days

Passing over the earth space,

My neurology, my spine, my limbs

The organs not failing me

Half a century-plus, still doing their chores

Yet another day devoured, concept and matter

I want a basket to gather days

Keep some days, discard others

Make a wager to trade bad for new

Where I didn't do this or say that

Yet days are to be inhabited, stretched into

They are all days, the only days

Days lived in beauty, and days lived in anger

Manahatta

Feet with crimson toe polish on the rails

I'm a balcony person now

Not a fire escape person

No watching people fast walk with Starbucks

My akimbo limbs melt on my balcony rail and chair

I half smile, feel the sun

Hold nothing, unconcerned about anyone

Before me is the Hudson, river of my life

The river that I cross by bridge now

I know this river newly

When its color changes

How the sun and moon caress its current

That the Lenape called it Mahicantuck

"The river that flows two ways"

Most days I see red-tail hawks

Some days I see light-foot deer beyond the trees

And as clearly as the river

The Chrysler Building also shines

The skyline of new towers

My Emerald City appears, a sparkling lullaby

A repository for horizontal sculpture

Ornamenting this two-way river

I see much, but I am the Unseen

A contemplator, a plotter of weekend deeds

I am apart and still a part

Of our bursting island

Of this mighty river

Today unencumbered like the fat moon

Soon sinking full into dreamscape Manahatta

Reckonings

Let it start
with the streetlamp at night
and leaning against it
and the push of bodies, so certain
that uncertain thoughts cannot betray
these bodies, so in focus
from the heat of you

Let it start there
and summon the smells
Invoke pungent sweat
from dancing hard
to erase and embrace everything
Thick in smoke and cologne
an opulent brew
and the moment is stretched out

But let it not stretch too long
for the bodies are eager

Where to go? Do we care?

How many words

for heat and madness?

Let it be tables and floors

and rooftops and subways

Let us push off the dawn

though it will push back

And that first morning

will be cataloged

into many mornings

Clothes thicken and soon

other people, jobs, relocations

mandates and precisions

Let it be a time neither then

nor now, and let it end

by a street lamp at night

Move towards the glow

from other pages

Inhale through years

Yesterdays crumble, tomorrows curve

Let it be a prayer

THREE

Flow

I am the mother, the witch, the huntress, the sage, the mystic, the lover

I am the lover, the mystic, the gatherer, the pagan, the daughter, the waif

I am the waif, the traveler, the healer, the explorer, the community worker

I am the worker, the soother, the disruptor, the raven, the wolf and the spider

I am the spider, the weaver, the worker, the lover, the sister, the peasant, the sorcerer

I am the sorcerer, the child, the crone, the disruptor, the crazy, the fortress, the leader

I am the leader, the needer, the sister, the misfit, the potential, the gift and the power

I am the power, the listener, the friend, the embracer, the giver, the taker

I sit by your side, link eyes, move with the movement

I'm water

Dispersion

At dinner, they pass dishes of pasta with a sauce of heart blood, plates of piled calamari, and sprinkles of nail clippings, black and bright orange. Their forms are familiar parallelograms, reflective as glass, their angles sharp and elongated. Eyelashes like tendrils. Lip gloss shooting out in bright colors colliding with blinding white light.

Below the ocean is a spectrum of colors. Fluorescents in the blackness of the deep. Breathing with gills, I plunge to find the big-brained octopus. The one with three hearts and eight brains. Graceful, delicate suctions explore the refinements of the seabed. I am shown the ocean's treasures: beings, shells, relics, worlds, and worlds within worlds. Schools of betta splendens and angelfish swarm for moments of fellowship. We hear the living coral sing. The octopus floats and shimmers, mimicking their colors.

At once, all eyes dart sideways, fish scatter, and the octopus's expression displays alarm, while her body turns a sickly gray. All eight tentacles, each with their brain, shoot behind her as if one. She springs forward in her waters. I struggle to swim alongside. From the dinner table, they are diving down, legs and acid laughter, pointing and trampling. My gentle companion shoots a great black cloud of ink. Her visage and theirs both dissipate. Blotted by the residue of the deep.

I am alone on the beach. I see stones of blue glass, pink and white shells and crabs scattering into their sand burrows. The seaweed is upon me. I feel my heart, three hearts: the beat of solitude, the beat of survival, the beat of receiving. The natural world is upon me. I am felt, seen, inhaled. The prism has shattered, and white light passes. Molecules reveal themselves deep in vibrational dance.

The Scents

Earth drapes us in fragrances

Each with their season

Jasmine and Gardenia

Slip into freedom

Reflection, recollection

Portals to possible worlds

Your finger entwined with mine

Let's linger in our mental paintings

Let the colors bloom, elated

Each scent is a daydream

A chord, a piano key

The scales of sacred aroma

Wish flowers, cradled by air

Aeronautic

"Hope is the thing of feathers"

My clipped wings grew back bright as a tiger

forged by anvil and fire

I soar above the leaping whales

with their triumphant spouts and spins

The thrill, the glide, the win

The soar and blaze and thrall of destination

My migration is to a higher vibration

Not carrying the weight others' ego trips, projections

Have you tried astral intervention?

Or words without body-guards and weapons?

Degrade another, degrade yourself

Clipped wings aim to steal sovereign nature

Caging, gauging, taking a wager

If you could see yourself through my eyes --

Flight brings a bird's eye view

I am off to better weather

Fly in beauty, just not together

the beaded women

beaded women dwell in walk-up studios, adobes, off-grid
or fireside, wrapped in the arms of *mi amor,* view of every
season
her eyes see you naked in conflict, in your sacred truth,
but past you, where all pantomime versions of the same
human tale

when beaded women gather, they emit animal laughs
dancing into moon space
tell embellished shero-journeys, filled in later
by inter-generational starlight

the beaded women of every culture
are neighborhood healers
regaling the lost, pointing towards grandeur or grace,
awaiting the question or action

come as you are, young or old,
seeking wisdom, queendom, queerdom, utopian dreams,
be warned of false friends,
avoid the key humming on the table

there is the loud rolling desert,

the silent rumination of city

the dancing of life connected beyond time

beyond technology, the false oracle of apple

beaded women dismantle oppression

perceive connections and interconnections

lose and find themselves in labyrinths

travel through time loops past the oppositional gaze

the seed of beads sprout fresh, rooted and reaching,

push beyond love pain,

bruises, shoves, anonymity

to inhale space between dread and beauty

beaded women love fire, flour, egg

pounding truth into bread dough

imagination birthed on Earth,

a soup and spice unique to every region

beaded women have bills,

take lovers, slam doors, go celibate,

collect mirrors for you or her

to bounce light – and transcend temporal reflection

raucous songs and soothing songs

nimble fingers crafting daisy chains,

reaching to link across every border

the adorned bounty of future grandchildrens' dreams

Dopamine Receptor

I recently noticed some strange activity

You did not initiate

There are settings to hold

Everything inside

Confirm name safeword password

Data might be compromised

There are ways to confirm suspicions

Maybe the next town

will have better directions

There's a diner with good coffee

and pancakes with real maple syrup

There is blue light for my hotspot

Two-way authentication needed

Promised Land

Time is gone
and the fog of my mind
is repossessed with burning
and the crevices in my bones
are filled with meadows
Bursting still, the wildflowers
marsh marigold and sarsaparilla
seen, grazed, inhaled
waiting alight, waiting for you

Make Me a Tree

The wind sings branches sway

Each leaf rustling as tambourines

A dance individual and collective

Their music, movement, the breeze, soothes the Hudson

Their food is the sun and summer rains

In turn life source for squirrels, birds, all winged beings

Life source for *all:* breathe the clean air

These ecosystems stretch before me

I smell fresh air cut with varied greens,

Time to leave my balcony, float downstairs,

Time to hug a tree

Trees are ancestors, root relatives

My cheeks rub rough bark

Secrets vibrate, trunk to ear

Mother Cosmos, make me a tree!

Wind for my strength, sap for my blood

The elemental art of photosynthesis

Absorbing and cleaning, prepared for each season

Upright and reaching, healthy for the world

Leilani

I meet a turkey at the sanctuary

Humans named her Leilani

She trots up to us at the entrance

And serenades us with turkey melodies,

Lively and purposeful

She coos,

"I am your tour guide

I know the best spots!

I'm down with the coolest goats,

the chillest pigs,

and I'm okay with the chickens,

But they're a bit cliquey,

not like us turkeys"

She keeps pace beside us

or just in front, chattering

Taking a decisive turn

Sharing her turkey point of view

I am compelled to kneel down and stroke her snowy
feathers
Leilani purrs, leans into the strokes
Pushing her warty head into my hand
Closing her gentle eyes
Then after this respite it was back to business
The human volunteer follows us haplessly
Leilani brings us to Nell the pig, who adores belly rubs
Leilani uses her limited flying ability to perch on the fence
and observe the interaction with satisfaction
She did Nell a solid

Towards the end of the tour the human drifts away
to answer another guest's questions about the rescued calf
and Leilani gives me a knowing side-eye/ don't-tell glance
Then dashes through a hole in a fence,
She bolts, running at 25 mile an hour, running like a badass
turkey bandit
When the human volunteer sees her, he sighs, frustrated
and amused
She escapes to where she laid her unfertilized eggs on the
DL
Like her hospitality, her parental instincts are strong
I'm told she does this when she thinks no one is looking

But she knows I saw

Maybe she views me as a turkey accomplice

Knows that I fell in love with Leilani at first sight

That I'd throw down for this turkey

This turkey, Leilani, is one kind and attentive turkey

A renegade turkey

People, don't underestimate a turkey

Ben Franklin didn't!

He thought wild turkeys should be the National Bird,

A preferable choice to the Bald Eagle

What if turkeys were the National Bird

Would we be eating Bald Eagles on Thanksgiving?

Known by Aztecs as the Jeweled Bird, the bred
domesticated turkey,

now looks pitiful. But in the spirit of the turkey is clever,
loyal and brave

Stroke a turkey, hug a turkey, hear the turkey purr, walk
and talk with a turkey

Earn the goddamn respect of a turkey!

Turkeys have lots of important turkey things to do

Now, this isn't a poem about factory farms or a vegan poem

It's not a poem about the 45 million plus turkeys slaughtered for Thanksgiving

It isn't about why Thanksgiving is a false narrative and a no-thanks

No! This poem is about Leilani the Sanctuary turkey

This is a poem about turkeys in general

That turkeys are cool birds

Turkeys are homies

Keep being you, turkeys!

Leilani, keep giving the best sanctuary tours

Keep being an exemplary inter-species conversationalist

Keep escaping the sanctuary to live the impossible dream!

Leilani, keep keeping hope alive,

Turkeys, keep on keeping hope alive

Beware of Artists

Beware of Artists

They will kill!

With their clay or paint or quill

Ignorance is a rusty train

Artists bring light, the speed, the rain

Beware of Artists

You will see

Defy ignorance and apathy

Beware of Artists

They twist and turn

They right their light

They sprout, they burn

No cliff too high nor speck too small

Artists are here to transform it all

Beware of Artists

We're everywhere

If you want to stay stuck

Best run from here!

Or become an Artist!

And you will see

Your own infinite alchemy!

Writing Beyond

I am writing beyond dystopia

Beyond capitalism

Beyond the patriarchy

Beyond colonialism

Beyond hegemony

Beyond binaries

I am writing beyond limitations

I am writing beyond war and crumbling societies

I am writing to survive

I am writing because love is in short supply

I am writing beyond supply and demand

I am writing because love is also imperfect

I am writing because words are often empty

I am writing to try and make them full

I am writing because after silence comes expression

I am writing in the cracks and through the layers

I am writing because time has been wasted

I am writing because I have lived too much

I am writing because I want to live more

I am writing because I am not yet defeated

I am writing because I am angry

I am writing because I am scared

I am writing to find today's power

I write pasts into futures

I write to revolutionize love

I write for animals, water, our planet

I write between the real and the imagined

I write to honor instruments, canvass, the body, the pen

I write as a woman

I write as I age with desire

I write my rage and my passion

For moments beyond this moment

I write to rattle the cage

To float in the ether of me

Remember

Remember the stars, the trees, the music,
the smile that caught you completely off guard?
The spontaneous laugh with a stranger!

We are shocked into zombie madness
Surrender to numbing routine
We learn our decrees and jurisdictions
Then build our doors and cages
We are taught the lives and deaths that matter
And we are taught those that do not

Remember when you walked with a person
that you never knew existed?
When you realize that your molecules
are not, in fact, your own?

I do
I remember
I remember you before you hurt me
I remember when I loved you and loved myself

I remember before I was alive

I remember when I was perfect

I remember you when you were glorious

I remember when we were not beyond hope

Do you see and remember yourself?

Do you remember when we both were different?

When the sun rose this morning, through the wind

I heard of the songs of you

Rubrics

The future fulfills through nature's temper

Through laws unfurling and obscuring thick smoke

Through the solitude of the elderly,

Through the blown minds of the young

Through the exhaustion of generations, cyclical songs

The panting of dying species still yearning to breed

For passionate idealism, there is always a need

The answers are documented, the promise proclaimed

Yet some holler: too fast, the market, the crash

Truth tellers and visionaries reviled, shrinking in shame

Or chanting ecstatic past safe keepers of tradition, taboo

Unshackle the mind,

Abandon the trickle of time

Teach and learn off the grid

Release the true selves that we hid

Watch the grass as it grows

Catch snowflakes while there is still snow

Acknowledgements

I want to express gratitude to my husband, F. Dean Hilmi, for listening to every poem and most revisions. Thanks for joining me at readings all over NYC and NJ. He cheers me in the crowd and serves as a muse.

Profound thanks to my mother, Gigi Bolt, still a busy theater professional, for taking the time to proofread. I also appreciate her enthusiasm, love and support.

Big props to Charles Gerbino for the cover photo. Please check out Charles' photos at artful_surfer on Instagram and his Facebook fan page. Thank you to Marina Obermaier for connecting me with Charles.

Thank you to my many supportive and inspiring colleagues. Thank you to writers Rich Ferguson, Lauri Maerov, Todd McKinney, M. Peach Robidoux and Jennie Wadworth for reading my work.

Here is to the poets and organizers who facilitate live and online readings. Your dedication and labors of love, create ripples, paths and bridges.

I enthusiastically thank my students for doing the scary work of digging deep to express themselves, for trusting, for creating and motivating each other and me.

Finally, hugs to Theo Bolt Moughalian, my beautiful and brilliant son, for sharing ideas, and for growing and learning together.

About The Author

Julie Bolt is an educator, poet, essayist and advocate for social and environmental justice. She's a tenured Associate Professor in English at Bronx Community College of the City University of New York. She received her interdisciplinary PhD in cultural studies from the University of Arizona. Her BA in creative writing is from Bard College. She also holds degrees from New Mexico State and Temple University.

Her creative and scholarly work has been published widely in print and online journals, and in anthologies. Her book on decolonial education is called *Border Pedagogy for Democratic Practice*. As part of her recent Andrew W. Mellon fellowship in Transformative Learning in the Humanities, her students produced a poetry podcast called *Counternarratives* on Spotify. She is currently founding 2Way River Lit, connecting NY and NJ poets with their shared literary histories and futures.

Although Julie has lived and worked in many states, she is originally a New Yorker from Greenwich Village and later a long time resident of Washington Heights. Currently, Julie resides in Fort Lee, NJ with her husband and cat Kazoo. She believes all arts are powerful tools for personal and social transformation.

563b6c13-f7f2-4fea-84a8-f6654bb03a1aR01